Francis Frith's

Lancaster Morecambe and Heysham

Photographic Memories

Francis Frith's
Lancaster Morecambe and Heysham

Cliff Hayes

Paperback edition first published in the United Kingdom in 2000 by
Frith Book Company Ltd

British Library Cataloguing in Publication Data

Francis Frith's Lancaster, Morecambe and Heysham
Cliff Hayes
ISBN 1-85937-233-3

Frith Book Company Ltd
Frith's Barn, Teffont,
Salisbury, Wiltshire SP3 5QP
Tel: +44 (0) 1722 716 376
Email: info@frithbook.co.uk
www.frithbook.co.uk

Printed and bound in Great Britain

Front Cover: Morecambe, West End 1899 42862

Acknowledgements
Thanks to the staff at the Lancaster museum for their help and co-operation.
Thanks also to Matthew Ashcroft for his knowledge of the villages, and the pubs in them.

AS WITH ANY HISTORICAL DATABASE THE FRITH ARCHIVE IS CONSTANTLY BEING CORRECTED AND IMPROVED AND THE PUBLISHERS WOULD WELCOME INFORMATION ON OMISSIONS OR INACCURACIES

Contents

Francis Frith: *Victorian Pioneer*

FRANCIS FRITH, Victorian founder of the world-famous photographic archive, was a complex and multi-talented man. A devout Quaker and a highly successful Victorian businessman, he was both philosophic by nature and pioneering in outlook.

By 1855 Francis Frith had already established a wholesale grocery business in Liverpool, and sold it for the astonishing sum of £200,000, which is the equivalent today of over £15,000,000. Now a multi-millionaire, he was able to indulge his passion for travel. As a child he had pored over travel books written by early explorers, and his fancy and imagination had been stirred by family holidays to the sublime mountain regions of Wales and Scotland. 'What a land of spirit-stirring and enriching scenes and places!' he had written. He was to return to these scenes of grandeur in later years to 'recapture the thousands of vivid and tender memories', but with a different purpose. Now in his thirties, and captivated by the new science of photography, Frith set out on a series of pioneering journeys to the Nile regions that occupied him from 1856 until 1860.

Intrigue and Adventure

He took with him on his travels a specially-designed wicker carriage that acted as both dark-room and sleeping chamber. These far-flung journeys were packed with intrigue and adventure. In his life story, written when he was sixty-three, Frith tells of being held captive by bandits, and of fighting 'an awful midnight battle to the very point of surrender with a deadly pack of hungry, wild dogs'. Sporting flowing Arab costume, Frith arrived at Akaba by camel seventy years before Lawrence, where he encountered 'desert princes and rival sheikhs, blazing with jewel-hilted swords'.

During these extraordinary adventures he was assiduously exploring the desert regions bordering the Nile and patiently recording the antiquities and peoples with his camera. He was the first photographer to venture beyond the sixth cataract. Africa was still the mysterious 'Dark Continent', and Stanley and Livingstone's historic meeting was a decade into the future. The conditions for picture taking confound belief. He laboured for hours in his wicker dark-room in the sweltering heat of the desert, while the volatile chemicals fizzed dangerously in their trays. Often he was forced to work in remote tombs and caves where conditions were cooler. Back in London he exhibited his photographs and was 'rapturously cheered' by members of the Royal Society. His reputation as a photographer was made overnight. An eminent modern historian has likened their impact on the population of the time to that on our own generation of the first photographs taken on the surface of the moon.

Venture of a Life-Time

Characteristically, Frith quickly spotted the opportunity to create a new business as a specialist publisher of photographs. He lived in an era of immense and sometimes violent change. For the poor in the early part of Victoria's reign work was a drudge and the hours long, and people had precious little free time to enjoy themselves. Most had no transport other than a cart or gig at their disposal, and had not travelled far beyond the boundaries of their own town or village. However, by the 1870s, the railways had threaded their way across the country, and Bank Holidays and half-day Saturdays had been made obligatory by Act of Parliament. All of a sudden the ordinary working man and his family were able to enjoy days out and see a little more of the world.

With characteristic business acumen, Francis Frith foresaw that these new tourists would enjoy having souvenirs to commemorate their days out. In 1860 he married Mary Ann Rosling and set out with the intention of photographing every city, town and village in Britain. For the next thirty years he travelled the country by train and by pony and trap, producing fine photographs of seaside resorts and beauty spots that were keenly bought by millions of Victorians. These prints were painstakingly pasted into family albums and pored over during the dark nights of winter, rekindling precious memories of summer excursions.

The Rise of Frith & Co

Frith's studio was soon supplying retail shops all over the country. To meet the demand he gathered about him a small team of photographers, and published the work of independent artist-photographers of the calibre of Roger Fenton and Francis Bedford. In order to gain some understanding of the scale of Frith's business one only has to look at the catalogue issued by Frith & Co in 1886: it runs to some 670 pages, listing not only many thousands of views of the British Isles but also many photographs of most European countries, and China, Japan, the USA and

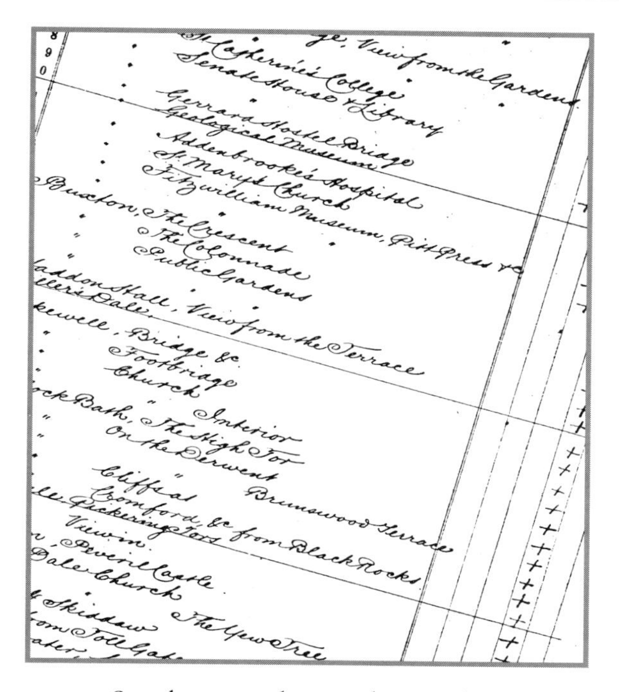

Catherine's College
Senate House & Library
Gerrard Hostel Bridge
Geological Museum
Addenbrooke's Hospital
St Mary's Church
Fitzwilliam Museum, Pitt Press &c
Buxton, The Crescent
The Colonnade
Public Gardens
addon Hall, View from the Terrace
ller's Dale
kewell, Bridge &c
Footbridge
Church
Interior
ck Bath, The High Tor
On the Derwent
Cliffs at Brunswood Terrace
Cromford, &c from Black Rocks
View in
Peveril Castle
Dale Church
Skiddaw
The Yew Tree
om Toll Gate

Canada – note the sample page shown above from the hand-written *Frith & Co* ledgers detailing pictures taken. By 1890 Frith had created the greatest specialist photographic publishing company in the world, with over 2,000 outlets – more than the combined number that Boots and WH Smith have today! The picture on the right shows the *Frith & Co* display board at Ingleton in the Yorkshire Dales. Beautifully constructed with mahogany frame and gilt inserts, it could display up to a dozen local scenes.

Postcard Bonanza

The ever-popular holiday postcard we know today took many years to develop. In 1870 the Post Office issued the first plain cards, with a pre-printed stamp on one face. In 1894 they allowed other publishers' cards to be sent through the mail with an attached adhesive halfpenny stamp. Demand grew rapidly, and in 1895 a new size of postcard was permitted called the court card, but there was little room for illustration. In 1899, a year after Frith's death, a new card measuring 5.5 x 3.5 inches became the standard format, but it was not until 1902 that the divided back came into being, with address and message on one face and a full-size illustration on the other. *Frith & Co* were in the vanguard of postcard development, and Frith's sons Eustace and Cyril continued their father's monumental task, expanding the number of views offered to the public and recording more and more places in Britain, as the coasts and countryside were opened up to mass travel.

Francis Frith died in 1898 at his villa in Cannes, his great project still growing. The archive he created continued in business for another seventy years. By 1970 it contained over a third of a million pictures of 7,000 cities, towns and villages. The massive photographic record Frith has left to us stands as a living monument to a special and very remarkable man.

Frith's Archive: *A Unique Legacy*

FRANCIS FRITH'S legacy to us today is of immense significance and value, for the magnificent archive of evocative photographs he created provides a unique record of change in 7,000 cities, towns and villages throughout Britain over a century and more. Frith and his fellow studio photographers revisited locations many times down the years to update their views, compiling for us an enthralling and colourful pageant of British life and character.

We tend to think of Frith's sepia views of Britain as nostalgic, for most of us use them to conjure up memories of places in our own lives with which we have family associations. It often makes us forget that to Francis Frith they were records of daily life as it was actually being lived in the cities, towns and villages of his day. The Victorian age was one of great and often bewildering change for ordinary people, and though the pictures evoke an impression of slower times, life was as busy and hectic as it is today.

We are fortunate that Frith was a photographer of the people, dedicated to recording the minutiae of everyday life. For it is this sheer wealth of visual data, the painstaking chronicle of changes in dress, transport, street layouts, buildings, housing, engineering and landscape that captivates us so much today. His remarkable images offer us a powerful link with the past and with the lives of our ancestors.

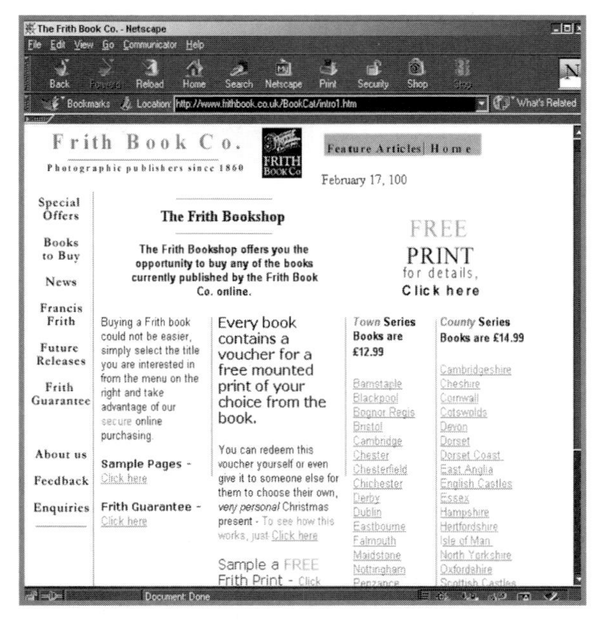

See Frith at www. frithbook.co.uk

Today's Technology

Computers have now made it possible for Frith's many thousands of images to be accessed almost instantly. In the Frith archive today, each photograph is carefully 'digitised' then stored on a CD Rom. Frith archivists can locate a single photograph amongst thousands within seconds. Views can be catalogued and sorted under a variety of categories of place and content to the immediate benefit of researchers.

Inexpensive reference prints can be created for them at the touch of a mouse button, and a wide range of books and other printed materials assembled and published for a wider, more general readership - in the next twelve months over a hundred Frith local history titles will be published! The day-to-day workings of the archive are very different from how they were in Francis Frith's time: imagine the herculean task of sorting through eleven tons of glass negatives as Frith had to do to locate a particular sequence of pictures! Yet the archive still prides itself on maintaining the same high standards of excellence laid down by Francis Frith, including the painstaking cataloguing and indexing of every view.

It is curious to reflect on how the internet now allows researchers in America and elsewhere greater instant access to the archive than Frith himself ever enjoyed. Many thousands of individual views can be called up on screen within seconds on one of the Frith internet sites, enabling people living continents away to revisit the streets of their ancestral home town, or view places in Britain where they have enjoyed holidays. Many overseas researchers welcome the chance to view special theme selections, such as transport, sports, costume and ancient monuments.

We are certain that Francis Frith would have heartily approved of these modern developments in imaging techniques, for he himself was always working at the very limits of Victorian photographic technology.

The Value of the Archive Today

Because of the benefits brought by the computer, Frith's images are increasingly studied by social historians, by researchers into genealogy and ancestory, by architects, town planners, and by teachers and schoolchildren involved in local history projects.

In addition, the archive offers every one of us an opportunity to examine the places where we and our families have lived and worked down the years. Highly successful in Frith's own era, the archive is now, a century and more on, entering a new phase of popularity.

The Past in Tune with the Future

Historians consider the Francis Frith Collection to be of prime national importance. It is the only archive of its kind remaining in private ownership and has been valued at a million pounds. However, this figure is now rapidly increasing as digital technology enables more and more people around the world to enjoy its benefits.

Francis Frith's archive is now housed in an historic timber barn in the beautiful village of Teffont in Wiltshire. Its founder would not recognize the archive office as it is today. In place of the many thousands of dusty boxes containing glass plate negatives and an all-pervading odour of photographic chemicals, there are now ranks of computer screens. He would be amazed to watch his images travelling round the world at unimaginable speeds through network and internet lines.

The archive's future is both bright and exciting. Francis Frith, with his unshakeable belief in making photographs available to the greatest number of people, would undoubtedly approve of what is being done today with his lifetime's work. His photographs, depicting our shared past, are now bringing pleasure and enlightenment to millions around the world a century and more after his death.

Lancaster Morecambe and Heysham

an Introduction

The area we cover in this book is one of the most fascinating areas in the whole North of England. Lancaster, with its river position and antiquity, is the centre of our attention, but the areas at every compass point out of Lancaster have a history all of their own, and also a different face for the visitor both today and in the past. They include the ancient village of Heysham and its unique St Patrick's chapel on the headland; Overton, a village where time seems to pass slowly; and Sunderland Point, where the tide, not traffic lights, controls the main road. To the north, we have Halton, once the capital of the area, and Bolton-le-Sands, an ancient cross-roads. Head west, and we are in Morecambe; go east, and we are in the back roads and quietness of Quernmore, once an ancient forest and hall. Glasson Dock and its industrial environment lies to the south-west, along with the ancient and almost deserted area around Cockersands Abbey.

Once the castle and courts of Lancaster had been established, the city became the judicial centre for every court in the area; even the Leet and Baron courts for Overton and the Forest Court for Quernmore were held at Lancaster. The parliamentary area of Lancaster stretched down as far as Fulwood.

The City of Lancaster

The ancient city of Lancaster gave its name not only to the Palatine County, but also to a royal house. The Tudors were descendants of the House of Lancaster, and the Duke of Lancaster was part of the Tudor dynasty.

The name of Lancaster's river was originally the Lon, meaning health-giving. The Roman name for fort, 'castra', became 'ceaster' in Anglo-Saxon, so the fort on the Lon became Lonceaster, and then over time Lancaster.

From Sunny Hill c1885 18083
Sunny Hill was south-west of the city near the Abraham Heights. Parts of Lancaster have some unusual names, including Primrose, Freehold and Marsh. The Priory tower, to the left, and the castle turrets dominated the skyline then just as they do now.

John of Gaunt

John of Gaunt's name is spoken of quite a lot in the city's history, but we are seldom told when he lived here or what was his connection with the throne. John was born in 1340 in Belgium, and was known as John of Ghent, but the name was anglicised. The title Earl of Lancaster was created for Edmund Crouchback, brother of Edward I. His grandson Henry had the title raised to Duke; when Henry's daughter Blanche married John of Gaunt, John took up the title Duke of Lancaster, and the land and power that went with it. (Royalty was marrying royalty: both John and Blanche were great-great-grandchildren of Edward I, and John was also the fourth son of Edward III). Blanche died in 1369; John then married Constanza of Castile - the marriage was an arranged one to calm things down in France. His brother the Duke of York married her sister Isabella; their children founded the House of York, which was to battle with the House of Lancaster in the War of the Roses. John of Gaunt became the power behind the throne of the young Richard II, who was only 6 months old when his grandfather Edward III died in 1377. He was ten years old when he was finally crowned. It was his uncle John of Gaunt who made most of the decisions during those years; John definitely had a hand in the introduction of a poll tax, and he prolonged the unpopular Hundred Years War against the French. The Peasants Revolt in 1381 was a protest against the policies that John had put in place as much as against Richard. When Henry Bolingbroke, the son of John of Gaunt, sided with powerful nobles to curb the king's power, he was banished from court; after his father John died in 1399, he was exiled. While Richard II was in Ireland, Henry raised an army of his own; before the king had returned, Henry and his supporters had taken power. Since he was a grandson of Edward III, parliament soon agreed to recognise him. Richard abdicated and died soon after at Pontefract, and Henry, the third Duke of Lancaster, became Henry I. The House of Lancaster had ascended to the throne, and the city of Lancaster had gained its royal connections, which are still enjoyed today.

The Town Hall 1886 18091

The old Town Hall was erected around 1781 on the site of an earlier town hall. Major Thomas Jarratt was the designer of the building, which opened in 1783. Market Square is the open area in front of the Town Hall, and Market Street runs to the left. The locals liked the large Tuscan portico and its four plain columns. The cupola and top were designed by Thomas Harrison, and were added just after the building opened. Harrison also designed Skerton Bridge. The total cost of the building was £2,054 13s 7d, including a £20 bonus that Mr Dickinson, one of the builders, had thought due to him.

◄ **The Park Footbridge c1885**
18098
Williamson Park was a gift from the Williamson family; it was begun by Joseph Williamson, and continued by his son (later Lord Ashton) in memory of his father. It was a magnificent gift, and is Lancaster's largest park. The Williamson family started making table baize, then known as American cloth, during the 1830s. They also made linoleum; they were at one time the largest manufacturer of this material, and exported it all over the world.

Church Street 1886 18092
We are looking down the street, away from the parish church, which gave the street its name. Church Street was never as busy or popular as Market Street. In Church Street stands the building (now the Conservative Club) where Bonnie Prince Charlie stayed twice in 1745. The first time was in October 1745, when he was heading south, full of hope and ready to regain the throne of England; the second time was in December 1745, when he was in retreat and heading north.

St Peter's Roman Catholic Cathedral c1885 18095
St Peter's is now one of Lancaster's great monuments. It was erected in 1859, just as the Roman Catholic faith was emerging from two hundred years of suppression. It has an imposing exterior with a 240ft spire, but its interior, with its statues and reliefs, is even more impressive. The relief of the Last Supper on the altar is beautifully executed, and the gilded roof and frescoes are outstanding.

From the Bridge 1891 28599
The River Lune and the town of Lancaster are viewed from the New Bridge, or the Skerton Bridge as it is now called. The bridge in our photograph is the Greyhound Road Bridge; it replaced the very first bridge, the medieval Old Bridge, which led directly to Bridge Hill and China Lane, which was only 8ft wide. This is the spot where the Romans built their ford to cross the River Lune; today the new Century Footbridge is being built here.

The Grammar School 1896 37373
Here we see the Grammar School from another angle, looking from East Road back into the city. Being on the far side of the Lancaster Canal from the centre, the school was considered to be out in the country, and the air was good for the boys. The building is still there today; it is now a Grant Maintained school. The tower of St Peter's Roman Catholic Cathedral can be seen in the background.

▲ **The Grammar School 1891** 28602
This is one of Lancaster's establishments which was allowed a Royal connection. Lancaster Royal Grammar School was founded in 1235, and in 1472 it was endowed by one John Gardyner. It moved to the site we see here on East Road in 1891, just before our photograph was taken.

▼ **The Royal Lunatic Asylum c1878** 10699
Built in 1816, the Lancaster Royal Lunatic Asylum had an average of over four hundred patients in the 1800s.

◄ **The Castle Gateway 1896** 37368
This is said to be one of the greatest castle entrances in England. Whether it was actually planned and paid for by John of Gaunt himself on one of his visits, or if it was erected in his memory after he died in 1399 is not very clear, but certainly it has borne his name for about six hundred years. The oak doors have slammed shut on some of the most fascinating names in history, including George Fox, the Lancashire Witches, and the priests and martyrs of the Reformation. John of Gaunt's image is above the door; it was he who had the courts and banqueting suite built within the castle.

The Castle, Shire Hall 1896 37370
Built in 1796-8 on the site of the original moat, the Shire Hall of Lancaster Castle is a fascinating building. It was built to do the business of the Shire; it contains over six hundred heraldic shields, and the coat of arms of every sovereign since Richard I. In the castle is a library, and in it is kept all the Laws of England since 1225. Court sittings permitting, we can tour the castle today and see much of this fascinating place, including the condemned cell, and an early gallows.

The Infirmary 1896 37378
The Royal Lancaster Infirmary is pictured in the year this building was opened by the Duke and Duchess of Gloucester, later to be George V and Queen Mary. Lancaster's first dispensary opened in 1781, established by Dr Campbell; there had been a small dispensary and a convalescent house in Lancaster before this. When the foundation stone of this building was laid in 1849 it was the start of Lancaster's first proper hospital. It is still there today, but is now surrounded by a mass and maze of the modern buildings that make up today's hospital.

Church Street 1896 37381
We are looking up Church Street towards St Mary's Parish Church and the Priory. The printing offices of the Lancaster Guardian was the second building on the right. Church Street was used as an open market on Lancaster Fair days. As the town was important, its Charter allowed four of these Fair Days - 3 April, 1 May, 5 July and 10 October, which was also the Winter Fair and Hiring Day. Lancaster's first Charter of 1199 gave Wednesday and Saturday as market days.

The Town Hall 1903 50057

We are in Market Square. The strange pole erected on the roof is the local telephone system. In the early years, all subscribers had their own separate line from the switchboard to their home or business. This led to a hundred or so separate wires heading over the roof-tops on poles and wooden constructions, as we see here. The Police Station and Fire Station, now the Library, are just on the right of the square. The corporation started making plans to move out of the old town hall as early as 1898, and bought a site in Dalton Square. It was over ten years later, in November 1910, that the staff moved out. The National Telephone Company were next door to the town hall, and they applied to pull it down, but were refused permission. Later, the ground floor of the building went to banking businesses, and the old council chamber became a museum. The museum grew considerably, and by 1977 it filled the whole building, as it still does today.

The Queen Victoria Monument 1912 64217

Lancaster's large, ornate Queen Victoria Monument must be one of the finest in the country. When the old Queen died after more than sixty years on the throne, England threw itself into the building of a plethora of monuments, each one trying to be better and different. Given by Lord Ashton in 1907, this one has Queen Victoria in bronze guarded by four bronze lions, symbols of Great Britain. In the panels below are the great Victorians who flourished during the Queen's long reign, including Lord Derby, Robert Peel, Cobden, Bright, Thackeray, Tennyson, and Lancaster-born Richard Owen; there are forty in all, with only two ladies, Florence Nightingale and Mary Ann Evans, who wrote under the name George Eliot. There are four corner pieces representing Truth, Wisdom, Justice and Freedom. The sculptor was Herbert Hampton. This monument was originally intended for Williamson Park, but after the Ashton Memorial was built there, it was decided to place the tribute to Victoria here. The building on the right, with a porch, is now a Yates's Wine Lodge, and next door at No. 2 was once the surgery of Dr Buck Ruxton, the infamous Lancaster murderer.

◄ **The Town Hall 1912** 64218
This fine view shows Lancaster's new town hall, seen from Dalton Square. The Town Hall, another gift from Lord Ashton, had opened in 1909; it was designed by E W Mountford, who was the architect of the Old Bailey in London. The building incorporated the Central Police Station, so there were cells and a Police Court as well as a Civic Hall. There are tours of the Town Hall, which is still a working centre for Lancaster. The local furniture makers Waring and Gillow provided the furniture for the building, and this in itself is worth viewing.

◄ **The Town Hall 1912** 64215
Here we have a clear view of Dalton Square, the Town Hall, and the Queen Victoria monument. It was in Dalton Square, named after the Dalton family, that the cattle and livestock markets were held when Market Square had proved too small. Lancaster Council had always intended to move its town hall here, and had already purchased the land for this purpose about fifteen years before the new town hall opened.

▼ **Williamson Park 1912** 64219
Williamson Park was begun in the late 1860s as a scheme for the unemployed; they were to turn the bleak moorland and the quarries, that had once provided so much stone for the building of Lancaster, into a charming and interesting park. Work improving the park carried on for over twenty-five years. It was James Williamson, who had made his money in linoleum, who paid for the park, and his son (also James), later Lord Ashton, carried on the support. Here we see the lake and fountain, and the Ashton Memorial towering over the landscape.

◄ **The Ashton Memorial 1912** 64220
When his second wife Jessie died, Lord Ashton, son of James Williamson, decided to erect a monument to her. The Taj-Mahal of Lancaster, it rises 220ft to dominate the highest spot over the city; its green copper domed roof stands out for miles. Work started in 1907, and the monument was complete in 1909. The Queen Victoria Monument was going to be built here, but it was re-directed to Dalton Square when plans for the Ashton Memorial were put forward. The Memorial fell into disrepair in the 1970s; restoration work started in 1984, and the Memorial re-opened to the public on 22 May 1987.

▼ The Church, from Cable Street 1912 64221

Cable Street is one of the older streets of Lancaster, though not one of the medieval streets. China Street, St Leonard's Gate, Penny Street, Church Street and Market Street formed the original layout of the town from 1610, as we can see from Speed's map of Lancashire, which had an inset showing the county's capital, Lancaster. The area captured in our picture is known as Fleet Square; beside the photographer is Water Street, which led to the early crossing-place of the River Lune.

▲ Lancaster from Skerton Bridge 1918 68329

▼ The River Lune, from Skerton Bridge 1918 68328A

This view from Skerton Bridge looks back down the River Lune to Lancaster. The bridge we can see here is a railway bridge built by the 'Little North Western', who constructed a line to Morecambe in 1849; their station was at Green Ayre. Our view clearly shows the terraced housing, built on the north side of the Lune outside the old city walls, where Lune Terrace and Derby Road are today.

◄ **The Cricket Ground 1918** 68330
Lancaster developed on the east slopes of the castle and church. This area was once called Kirk Lancastre. All the buildings of early and medieval Lancaster were in the area in front of the castle gateway. This left the area behind the castle free for development, and open spaces and industrial buildings appeared in the mid Victorian period. Our photograph was taken from Giant Axe Field; the area behind the photographer, known as Marsh, had at the time been developed as a linoleum and oilskin manufacturing plant.

The River Lune 1918 68331
Here we see the River Lune just before it passes the ancient city. The area known as Beaumont lies across the river, and the Skerton Bridge is in the distance. The Skerton Bridge was built in about 1783 by a consortium of builders (including many of the Muschamp family), and cost £14,000. The designer was Thomas Harrison, whose plan for a flat bridge with open spaces over the piers of the bridge was soon copied all over England. Boating was popular on this stretch of the river, and rowing boats could be hired by the hour.

The War Memorial 1925 77913
A winged angel guards this tribute to the 'Honoured Memory of the Men of Lancaster Who Gave Their Lives in the Great War 1914-18'. This is not the only tribute to the fallen heroes; there is also a bronze statue by Jennie Delahunt of two soldiers sharing water, and round it there were cottages built for the returned heroes in a 'village' designed by Thomas Mawson.

The View from the Castle 1927 80504

We are looking over Lancaster and the outer parts of the castle from the higher inner ramparts. This large, square Norman keep with its 10ft-thick walls was restored on orders from Queen Elizabeth I. We can see the round tower added by King John, and the back of the famous John of Gaunt Gateway; the Ashton Memorial, looking like St Paul's in London, stands out from the murk of Lancaster behind. Part of the courtyard below was used to bury victims who were hung publicly outside the castle walls. This was especially true of Catholic priests, who were hung, drawn and quartered; to prevent their remains being dug up and taken away, all the bits would be buried separately.

◄ **A Castle Warden 1927** 80507
One of the castle's wardens stands on the 10ft-thick keep walls and points out something of interest to the visitors. One of the fascinations of Lancaster Castle is this mix of historic building and its use as a court and jail today. This gives an added interest to visitors; they learn that while they are being shown round the old cells and the Shire Hall, someone is sitting in the cells nearby working out where they went wrong in life. While the visitors shudder at the gallows and 'drop room', someone nearby is working on family visits for a person on remand, locked up in this very same building. The tower behind our warden is John of Gaunts tower. This is the beacon point for the castle, and would have been used to signal the sighting of the Spanish Armada.

▲ **From Castle Hill c1950** L10007
We are looking down Castle Hill, by the wall of Lancaster Castle. St Mary's Promenade is to the left, going up to the church. The Judge's Lodgings are at the bottom of Castle Hill down the lane. It would be up this walk that the Assize Judge and his entourage would walk on Assize Court days; the judge's man would carry the black cap used for passing the sentence of death. At the bottom of the lane you can just make out Covell's Cross, which stands outside the Judge's Lodgings: here the Kings and Queens of England have been proclaimed. The Lodgings are now the Gillow Museum of Furniture and a Museum of Childhood.

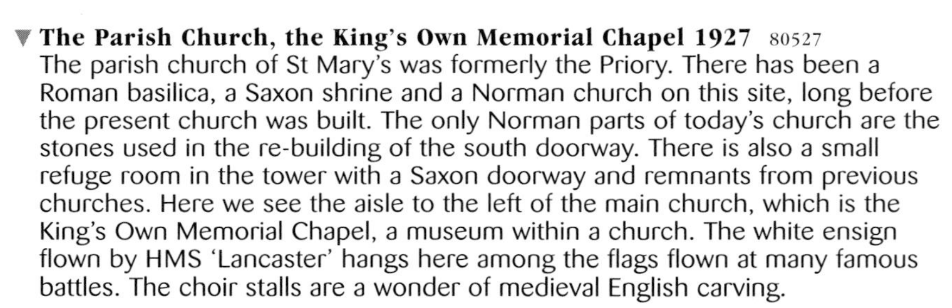

▼ **The Parish Church, the King's Own Memorial Chapel 1927** 80527
The parish church of St Mary's was formerly the Priory. There has been a Roman basilica, a Saxon shrine and a Norman church on this site, long before the present church was built. The only Norman parts of today's church are the stones used in the re-building of the south doorway. There is also a small refuge room in the tower with a Saxon doorway and remnants from previous churches. Here we see the aisle to the left of the main church, which is the King's Own Memorial Chapel, a museum within a church. The white ensign flown by HMS 'Lancaster' hangs here among the flags flown at many famous battles. The choir stalls are a wonder of medieval English carving.

◄ **The Castle c1950** L10029
The railings have gone from round the grassy area to the left, next to Castle Park. It was this cobbled spot that played host to the public hangings that sometimes took place here in Lancaster. The last public hanging took place in 1865, less than a hundred years before our photograph. Note the floodlights on the grass on the right to light the Gateway at night, and to help with security.

▼ **From the Castle c 1950** L10039
We are looking down from Castle Park to Castle Hill and the city beyond. The Ashton Memorial can be seen on the skyline at the other side of the city, in the centre of the picture. The Tourist Information Centre is now in the smallish square house at the bottom of the hill. The Castle gateway is out of shot on the left.

▼ **Market Street c1950** L10038
This is the very top of Market Street as we turn out of Castle Hill. The road coming in 100 yards down on the right is King Street, the A6 and the original road north; we can see that even fifty years ago it was one-way (note the no entry signs), showing that Lancaster had traffic problems even then. The Post Office and the King's Arms Hotel on the right are still there today. The King's Arms now has a gentle, unchanged air about it, though the area to the left, by the telephone box, is a Cafe Wine Bar with an open-air area outside.

▲ **Market Street c1950**
L10042
We can see the old town hall with its apex roof peeping out on the left hand side, 100 yards up the street. Now a museum, it includes among its collection all the charters granted to Lancaster. The Tetley sign on the right of the street marks the John of Gaunt Hotel, which is still there today; it has plenty of character and eccentricity (as well as decent food and real ale).

◄ **Penny Street c 1950** L10044
This is one of Lancaster's main shopping streets. Chris Williams' radio shop is first on the right; in country districts, the radio, with its BBC Home and Light programmes, helped people to keep in touch. Lancaster is on the edge of the Lake District, and an important point on routes both north and south. The National Cyclists Union and others would recommend a stop such as the 'Cyclists Rest' Bed & Breakfast, on the left above Babyland. Note the ornate light suspended above the street - no need for lamp posts in this busy road. Compare this light with the new sodium street lights suspended in the photograph above.

Market Square c1955 L10049

Here we see the Square outside the old town hall and part of Market Street. At this time, Market Square was a bus station; we can see the bus shelters on the left. Also evident is the underground toilet, which is one amenity that needs to be looked at seriously and improved in most northern towns and cities. The van on the right, outside the Palace Picture House, looks like a Lune Laundry's van, a local company who expanded all over Lancaster and to Manchester and Liverpool. The Blue Anchor Hotel is seen on the left. Today, if you go down the passage next to Bradley's, you enter a lovely indoor courtyard, part of the hotel's complex. It has memorabilia and reminders of Lancaster's maritime past, and provides a pleasant respite from the world of shopping that Lancaster provides.

Morecambe

The seaside town of Morecambe, situated on Morecambe Bay, has wonderful views of the hills of the Lake District. The brine-tinged air from the bay, softened by the fresh air flowing in from across the Lake District, produced what Morecambe does best - a relaxing and exhilarating environment for a break or holiday. The whole area has been designated one of Outstanding Natural Beauty, and the Bay itself is one of Europe's best habitats for migrating birds.
Much maligned, Morecambe has always had to compete with other Lancashire seaside towns, and this does show in its history. The town started life as Poulton; then, to avoid confusion with another Poulton near Blackpool, it became Poulton-le-Sands - the other was Poulton-le-Fylde. Poulton-le-Sands is mentioned in the Domesday Book. The ancient fishing village of Bare was just to the north of Poulton, and was the home of the famous Morecambe Bay Shrimpers. Poulton-le-Sands, Bare and Torrisholme came together to form Morecambe around 1860, although the area had already started to develop as a seaside resort when the railway arrived in around 1849.

Morecambe, The Esplanade 1888 21076
This early photograph shows the front at Morecambe over 110 years ago. Local fishermen used their boats to offer trips round the bay, which supplemented their income from catching shrimps and mussels. When the summer visitors arrived, some of the boats would be spruced up so as to turn to catching holiday-makers instead of fish.

Morecambe, The Sands 1888 21078

'The sands', says the Frith title, but as you can see, central Morecambe has always had a pebble beach, especially at high tide. The stone jetty that we can see in the background was the main terminal for ships to Ireland and the Isle of Man, until Heysham Harbour was cut in the 1900s. The broad, stone-built jetty included sheds as shelter for passengers, as well as loading and unloading facilities, and trains could also back onto the pier, as we see in our photograph. Bathing machines are still in evidence at the edge of the water in this picture, and Morecambe was the proud possessor of about twenty of them when our photograph was taken. Locals always referred to them as 'vans'.

◄ **Morecambe, The Pier 1888** 21080
There were two piers at Morecambe in the past. This one is the Central Pier, opened in 1869 to give visitors and holiday-makers a change - they could walk over the water and look down on the sea. When the pier first opened, there were no buildings or pavilions at the end. Holiday-makers staying the week could purchase a weekly ticket for only a shilling (5p), and stroll over the water for a full seven days.

Morecambe, The South End 1896 37386
The southern part, towards Heysham, soon developed as the more genteel side of the resort, with smart hotels; it was thought to be a little superior. The area today is known as Sandylands. Our horse tram is wending its way from Upper Heysham back to Morecambe. Today there is a very popular walk along the promenade between Morecambe and Heysham.

Morecambe, West End Pier 1896 36387
In 1896, Morecambe opened a second pier, known as West End Pier, which is the one we see here in our picture. The building of a lavish pavilion at the end of this pier motivated the Central Pier to build a theatre at the end of their pier. The West End Pier was destroyed in a storm in November 1977; it was declared unsafe, and was demolished soon after.

Morecambe
The Central Pier and the Esplanade 1899 42857
This lovely view of the Promenade looks south towards Heysham, with the Central Pier in the background. Central Pier reacted in grand style to the opening of the West End Pier by building a pavilion at the end. It soon gained the nick-name 'the Taj Mahal', and indeed it did resemble that famous building. This Indian Pavilion burnt out in a fire in 1933; it was rebuilt in 1935, but it was not as grand as the original.

Morecambe
The Promenade 1899
42855
This is a busy scene. Walking and strolling, and taking in the sea air, was what the late Victorian holiday-makers demanded. Resorts from Morecambe down the coast through New Brighton to Llandudno in Wales provided the wide walk-ways where holiday-makers could stroll and pass the time of day with family and friends away from the traffic. Note all the traffic in this picture is horse-drawn.

Morecambe
The Promenade 1899 42860
The pier, the sea, bracing air and excursions to Heysham and the Lakes - that was what the holiday-makers wanted, and that was what Morecambe provided. Because of its closeness to the northern border, it always had a 'Scotch Week' when workers from Glasgow and the surrounding area would descend and 'let loose'. It was a sort of Wakes Week, Scottish style; it was always in mid-July.

Morecambe
West End Pier 1899 42867
At the turn of the 20th century, late Victorians enjoy a walk above the water on West End Pier. The spaces between the planks meant that you could see the water below, and this added to the excitement and danger of the early piers.

◀ **Morecambe West End 1899** 42862
The southern part of Morecambe was always referred to as the West End. Here we see the exclusive part of Morecambe, and our view takes in Morecambe Tower. Every resort wanted a copy of the Eiffel Tower, and Morecambe was no exception. The tower here was started around 1895, just after Blackpool's, but it was never finished. Our view shows what working-class people did for their week's holiday: they sat and relaxed and took in the sea air.

▲ **Morecambe, West End Promenade 1899** 42864
The Morecambe tower has grown higher in this later view. Again, horses are very prominent in our photograph: one brave horse cab is going through the waves, and horses from the 'vans' (bathing machines) are coming ashore. There would have been about one thousand people in Morecambe whose employment was looking after or working with the horses of the town at this time.

◀ **Morecambe The Front 1899** 42868
The town's Eiffel tower has reached a third of its eventual height, and there is a viewing platform in use at this time. The building to the right of our picture is the Victoria Buildings, which was put up and named in honour of Queen Victoria in her Jubilee Year, 1887.

Morecambe
The Sands 1899 42870
Our late Victorian visitors were presented with a pebbly beach. We can see the stone jetty in the distance: it was still the main anchorage for ships when our photograph was taken. The just-paddling brigade stayed south of the Stone Pier, which was still a busy working port. It would continue to be so until Heysham opened in around 1904. The jetty was later rented to T W Wards, a ship breakers, and became quite a visitor attraction, with ships moored waiting to be broken up. In the years after the First World War, nearly half a million people paid to tour the ships waiting for the breakers' torch.

Morecambe
West End Promenade 1903 50061
Here we see the area at the start of the West End Pier. By the beginning of the 20th century, Morecambe had most of its major attractions in place, things that would bring in the visitors for many years. The two piers were completed, and so was the promenade, complete with free shelters; there was a fun fair, and in 1890 Morecambe started an annual Music Festival, which was very popular. The tower, though, was never completed - it might otherwise have lasted longer than to 1912, when demolition started. We can see the part-completed tower on the sky-line. It seems to have lost its viewing platform by the time that this photograph was taken.

Morecambe
Central Promenade 1906 56104
This is the area which was at the entrance to Central Pier; at this time it was the centre for visitors in Morecambe. This is reflected by the number of dining rooms we can see on our photograph. As well as the Star Dining Rooms and the Pier Head Dining Room on its left, we have another on the very right of our view. The Queen's Hotel is just to the right of the clock tower; it was one of the resort's main hotels at this time. If we look closely, we can see the tower still peeping over the rooftops on the left.

Morecambe
The Tower Building from Central Promenade c1950 M94008

The buildings beneath the tower were completed at the turn of the 20th century. Just like Blackpool today, our tower building contained a theatre (later a cinema), a ballroom and gardens. When the tower itself came down in about 1912, the tower building continued to be a centre for entertainment. About this time it was renamed the Gaumont and became a cinema, but it closed in 1959. It then became a ten pin bowling alley through the 'swinging sixties', and then a bingo hall. The building is still there today, but plans and ideas for its future seem to change with every tide.

◄ **Morecambe Central Pier 1906** 56106

The pavilion seen in our photograph was built in 1897 to dwarf the West End Pier dome that had just been completed. Locals soon found a nick-name for our end-of-the-pier Victorian edifice. They called it 'the Taj Mahal of Morecambe', and it was a wonderfully eccentric and ornamental building until it was burnt down in 1933.

▼ **Morecambe, The Clock Tower c1950** M94014

Our clock tower is showing signs of age in this photograph from half a century ago. The marked two colours of brick are not so easy to distinguish fifty years on from our earlier photographs. The ornate clock tower was a gift to the town in 1905 from Alderman J R Birkett.

◄ **Morecambe West End Promenade c1950** M94019

We are looking at the area that was between West End and Central Piers just before they both fell foul of the weather. The fair had grown and developed, and the council had opened Happy Mount Park (in 1927) to give holiday makers an even more memorable holiday. The Clarendon, on the right, was an old-established hotel.

WINTER GARDENS
INFORMATION BUREAU

Morecambe Central Promenade c1950 M94023
This view shows a mixed bag of transport. The horse carriages, which were a popular tourist taxi, are present at the head of Central Pier, while the post-war growth in the car industry is reflected in new and pre-Second World War cars. The number of motor bikes and side-cars parked here shows how popular that form of transport really was in the 1950s and 1960s. The large building on the left is Morecambe Winter Gardens, opened in 1878 as 'the People's Palace of Varieties & Aquarium'. It had been enlarged in 1897-98 and re-named the Victoria Pavilion. The theatre inside could hold around 4,000 people at each show.

◄ **Morecambe, The Start of West End Pier c1955** M94052
Jugs of tea are advertised on the left, and 'Walkie Photos' on the right. It is a pity that more effort was not put into saving one of Morecambe's piers in the late 1970s when they were still there; but those years were not a time when conservation or heritage featured much on the agenda. The Super Swimming Stadium had opened in 1936; as a promotion for the pool, a Miss Great Britain competition was started in Morecambe in 1945. In 1964 Marineland, Europe's first Oceanarium, opened on the old stone jetty.

◄ **Morecambe, Central Beach c1950** M94022
Holiday-makers cling on to a small piece of beach at high tide. They seem to be mostly mothers and their young children, which exemplifies Morecambe's family image. The fancy Victorian shelters along the promenade have gone, but there is still one of the old wooden jetties, which were put up by local fishermen for loading trippers onto their boats for trips round the bay. On the far right of our picture we can see the Midland Hotel, built in Art Nouveau style to a design by Oliver Hill in 1933. Today, the hotel is the centre of much attention and preservation orders.

▲ **Torrisholme, The Shopping Centre c1965** T238014
Here we see the centre of Torrisholme, a quiet Morecambe suburb, on a pleasant, sunny day. The Domesday Book recorded life as it was in these parts all those centuries ago, and today we sometimes find it hard to realise that this area around Halton and Lancaster was an important and busy working area; Liverpool and Manchester were still insignificant places, and hardly got a mention. Torrisholme was recorded as Toredholme, and later still as Toroldesbi. The George Hotel is on the right, next to Shaw's shop. In 1965 Torrisholme was developing as a place to live for people working in Morecambe or Lancaster; from here they could easily commute to work.

◄ **Torrisholme, A Wagonette at the George Hotel c1965** T238026
This 'Happy Days' wagonette or country-style horse bus, harking back to transport in earlier days, is taking a party on a jaunt on a sunny day. Our photographer was lucky to catch the party who pose happily for him. They are probably regulars from the hotel, and are going on a specially-organised day out. Torrisholme was once a hamlet two miles north-west of Lancaster, and was one of the three villages which combined with Bare and Poulton-le-Sands to make up Morecambe around 130 years ago.

Heysham

Heysham is a very ancient village, that can easily trace its history over 2,000 years. At one time there were two separate communities, Heysham Village, lower down, and higher Heysham around Heysham Hall, now an hotel. The fact that the village name is first recorded in the Domesday Book as Hessam leads historians to believe that the name comes from an early low German personal name, 'Hess'. The 'y' element did not come into the name until the middle 1600s. The spelling of the village name has changed a few times since it was first written: Heseym (1094), Hescam (1222) and Hesame (1463) are some of the variations. The other Heysham is the new harbour, opened at the very start of the 20th century in about 1903; there was also the famous Heysham Holiday Camp next to the harbour, known in the 1960s as Middleton Towers.

Heysham Parish Authorities came under the barony of Lancaster and the Poor Law Union of Caton. They ran the area until they were succeeded by the Heysham Urban District Council in 1899. The UDC amalgamated with Morecambe in 1928.

Heysham, The Village 1895 35868
This charming view of the village of Heysham was taken from the cliff walk leading to Sandylands and Morecambe. At the time, tourism would support the village in the summer, and fishing in the winter months. We can see that the footpath is a well-worn one, so it must have been popular with visitors. The cliffs at Heysham are the first coming north after the Great and Little Orme at Llandudno; they presented the Victorian visitor with breathtaking views over to the Lake District.

▼ **Heysham, The Church 1888** 21072
The origins of the parish church of St Peter on Heysham Head are lost in the mists of time. The earliest recorded date is 1080, when it was noted as an old Saxon church. There was probably an earlier church on this site, built by the Angles. Quite a bit of the Saxon stonework remains today, even though the church has been added to and enlarged. The original part is at the centre. Note the lack of standing gravestones in the graveyard around the church.

▲ **Heysham Head, St Patrick's Chapel Ruins 1888** 21071
St. Patrick himself is said to have been shipwrecked on the head; years later, monks came from his monastic foundation in Ireland and built this chapel in his memory. It dates from Saxon times, the 8th century, and one of the reasons it had stood so long in such an exposed spot is the mortar. It is ground-up sea shells, heated and mixed with boiling water to give a cement-like substance. It is the only example left in England of a single-cell Saxon chapel. Originally it was 24ft x 8ft, with walls nearly 3ft thick. Our Victorian ladies posing by the chapel add charm to our photograph - which apart from them could have been taken today.

▼ **Heysham, St Peter's Church, South Side 1892** 30443
We are looking at the leeward side from the entrance to the churchyard. Note how many standing headstones there are now, only four years after picture No 21072. We can clearly see the 1864 extension, the lower part to the right with its own small entrance. This end of the church is in three parts, as we can tell by the three apex roofs. Today, when we visit this area around the altar and choir, we will find a wonderful small intimate part of the church cut off from the chancel by an oak screen, believed to have come from Cockersands Abbey. The vicar from 1865 to 1900 was the Rev Charles Twemlow Royds, whose family owned the advowson (or right of patronage).

◄ **Heysham, Stone Coffins 1912** 64229

These unique and mysterious stone coffins (ossuaries) are near St Patrick's chapel. Anything we say about these resting places cut into the rock is purely speculation. There are six here, and two more over by the chapel door. They were cut in the Dark Ages with primitive instruments, and my thoughts are that they have been used more than once. I think the Vikings may have plundered and thrown out the original corpses, and they were used again when Christianity was restored. Carbon tests on the bones found in the coffins date from the 900s, yet the coffins are much, much earlier. The fence round the chapel and the barbed wire round the coffins is very surprising. Today, there are no fences up on the head - not even one to keep one away from the edge.

▼ **Heysham, The Parish Churchyard, the Hogback Stone 1912** 64232
This stone, which marked the grave of a Viking warrior, marked his resting spot for over 1,000 years: it is from the 10th century. (Note the barbed wire again around the historical artifact at the time when our picture was taken). He had converted to Christianity; but though one side of the stone is carved with Christian symbols, the other side represents the pagan Viking heaven. In 1961 it was taken inside the church for protection against the weather and against too many visitors running their hands over the stone. Though there are other hogback stones, this is the finest and best preserved.

▼ **Heysham, The Shoreline and Fairy Chapel Rocks 1912** 64233
The rocky coast around Heysham Head provided excitement and danger for its Victorian and Edwardian visitors. No holiday in Morecambe or Lancaster was complete without a day at Heysham. Nicknames or folk names gave places added attraction to those day-trippers; here we see the rock formation known for many years as 'The Fairy Chapel'. Our two visitors seem impressed enough to pose for their photograph.

▲ **Heysham, The Foreshore c1947** H81003
Post-war visitors gather and take in the fresh sea air on the rocky shore. The car is making its mark on leisure time, and petrol was available again after the war-time restrictions. Even then, parking in the village was a problem; these visitors have chosen to chance leaving their cars, motor bikes and motor bikes and sidecars on the rocky beach. I hope they know when the tide is due in. King George, as Duke of Lancaster, owned the foreshore here. I wonder if he charged for parking then?

Heysham, Main Street 1947 H81005
This charming view looks up Main Street from the shore. I find the wooden posts erected to mark out the gardens of the row of houses on the left fascinating. These would stop visitors peering through the windows, and give the inhabitants a little bit of privacy. A photographer waits to snap visitors; I wonder if he developed the prints in an hour - the slogan used to be 'pick up before you leave'. The Royal Hotel on the right, half-way up Main Street, is still there; like the village, it seems to have resisted change and modernisation. It is still today a lovely mish-mash of small rooms and cosy bars, and when last visited (September 2000) was still serving mild beer.

Heysham
The Village 1947 H81006

We are at the top of Main Street, looking back down through the village from the bus station. Traffic will always be a problem to the small fishing village, and here we see the two old buildings which make the Main Street entrance narrow and restrict traffic. Charabancs, coaches, omnibuses and so on have always had to park at the top of the street and let the visitors wander down. Nettle beer, once sold from every house in the village, can now only be obtained from the Curiosity Corner Cafe, which is on the very left of our photograph. The large square building on the right had for many years a large brass weighing machine outside. For 6d the showman would 'Guess Your Weight'. You got your money back if he was not within 2-3lbs of your real weight when he weighed you straight afterwards.

Heysham
Cosy Corner c1900

The popularity of Heysham, as far as visitors are concerned, has waxed and waned over the last 150 years since the coming of the railway. At the present time, Heysham seems to be climbing out of the doldrums of the early 1990s, and is pushing itself forward. I do not think anyone wants a return to 1900, when around 1,000 visitors would arrive on a reasonable day; they would spend the time walking the head, visiting the gardens and, of course, taking lunch or afternoon tea. The house in our photograph is on the left just as you enter Main Street, and it still has the date outside. At the time of this photograph, it was Mrs Kellett's Tea Rooms, but it is a private house today.

Heysham
The Foreshore c1950

The shore line at Heysham is owned by Queen Elizabeth II. The concrete sea defence to Morecambe has been constructed, and provides a sort of primitive promenade. Can you make out the concrete terraces that have been constructed on each side of the village slipway? As the tide is in, they are full of visitors in our photograph; the pebble beach is covered, so we see only the sandy bit of Heysham.

Heysham, Cosy Corner c1900 H81301

Heysham, The Foreshore c1950 H81002A

Heysham, Heysham Tower 1915 H81014
Heysham Tower was built by T J Knowles in about 1837, and it was the home of the Cawthra family. There was a lodge down in the village, and the estate of about 14 acres was laid out with attractive gardens and woods. When construction started on Heysham Harbour, the family moved out; it was bought by the Midland Railway, who were building the harbour. At the time of our photograph it was an hotel. In 1925 it became the Morecambe Bay Holiday Camp, with 400 campers in this building and another 100 men in permanent tents in the grounds. It later became Middleton Towers Holiday Camp.

Heysham, Half Moon Bay c1965 H81027
It is a busy beach in the Swinging Sixties: these people are not day trippers to Heysham, but guests of Middleton Towers who have made their way to the beach for a day of free activity and entertainment. The holiday complex and Tower buildings are still standing; over the last decade since they closed, it has been proposed that they could be used as a Vietnamese boat people's village, an illegal immigrants centre, an open prison and a Yugoslavian refugee camp.

Heysham, The Docks c1915 H81009
Once built, the docks at Heysham were popular and well-used. In 1909 the South Jetty was built, and this protected the deep-water channel used by the larger ships. Here we see one of the four steamships built by Midland Railways to get the most out of the Heysham/Ireland route. The white band of the funnel which marked Midland Railway ships is also reflected in the tugs across the harbour, also owned by the Midland Railway.

Douglas, Victoria Pier 1907 59160
In the years just after it opened, almost 50% of the passenger traffic from Heysham Harbour went to Douglas, Isle of Man. Heysham was a popular port with Yorkshire people, who found it easier to get to than Liverpool, Fleetwood and Holyhead, even further away. Here we see one of the Midland Railway ships tied up at Douglas's Victoria Pier, along with a mixed collection of steam ships and paddle steamers. The crossing from Heysham was the shortest of all the crossings, and in 1907 it would take four hours.

Douglas
From Douglas Head 1907 59152

Heysham became the centre for travel to the Isle of Man, and in 1923 the Fleetwood services were transferred there. 'Scotch Week' saw passenger numbers double, and Yorkshire Wakes Weeks kept the port busy. At this time the Isle of Man was a superior holiday venue, definitely something to mention in your circle of friends. If you went there, it meant that you had crossed the water, taken a little more effort, and almost gone abroad for your holiday. Here we see the Midland Railway ship 'Antrim' in Douglas Harbour, waiting to return to Heysham.

Glasson Dock

In 1780 the River Lune was silting up. The dock that had been established at Sunderland Point by Robert Lawson was having problems getting goods into and out of Lancaster, governed as it was by a tidal highway. Lancaster's solution was to build a dock near the village of Glasson.
Work began in 1783, and by 1790 the quays were in use; a year later, it was a fully operational port. Though it solved Lancaster's problems of import and export, it did nothing to improve her communications with the growing industrial heart of Lancashire to the south. The Lancaster Canal Company was formed in 1787, but it was 1819 before the canal to Preston opened. In 1826 the branch to Glasson Dock was completed, and the river and dock were connected to the canal system and Lancaster. The Glasson Dock branch, just three and a half miles with six locks, was the most important section of the Lancaster Canal as far as most Lancaster merchants were concerned.

Glasson Dock c1950 G244004
This is the main dock which gave its name to Glasson Dock, with a sailing ship tied up. The hotel on the corner was called Gerrard's at the time. The name Glasson is one of those names that historians dislike, because there is no known explanation for it. Old Norse has 'glas' meaning a river, so it could be 'the place on the river' - but that would be written 'Glason'. The first recorded mention of this tiny fishing community set on Fishnet Point was in 1587, and that was as Glasson.

Glasson Dock c1955 G260026
After the turn of the 19th century, Glasson Dock was used more and more by pleasure craft. Wealthy mill owners and industrialists found it handy to leave their boats in the shelter of the dock or the canal basin, and leisure became more and more a source of income for Glasson Dock. Here we see only two working ships to four pleasure cruisers, though ships could only come and go into the dock on a rising or high tide. Our hotel has had a big facelift: it stands out white and ornate in Victoria Terrace, which contains a pub at either end.

◄ **Glasson Dock c1955** G260003
This view shows the main dock, with the River Lune beyond. Our photographer is standing on the bridge over the lock which separates the dock from the Lancaster Canal basin. At the time of our photograph, ship repairing was still going on at Glasson, and the graving or dry dock was still in use. We see behind the dock a busy little port, though it was mostly used by coasters and Irish cargo boats.

▼ **Glasson Dock Victoria Terrace c1955** G260011
We can take a closer look at that terrace. Our hotel is now called the Caribou, a strange name for a hotel in a small port in Lancashire. You cannot go in and ask why, as it is all boarded up and to let today. On the right you can see the Nissen huts put up in the 1939-45 war for soldiers and the Home Guard, who were based here to keep supplies flowing during the war years. This area is now the main car park for visitors. One of the gondolas from the big wheel at Blackpool ended its life as a cafe here, and stood just to the right of our picture.

◄ **Glasson Dock The Quay c1955** G260012
We are actually inside the port area here; again we see the mixture of coasters, fishing vessels, yachts and pleasure craft. Even today the dock is like a living open-air museum, with old bits of machinery and rusting equipment around. Though the railway here closed in 1964 along with Condor Green Station, there are still lines and the odd wagon in the dock. The area around Glasson is teaming with wildlife, and is a bird watcher's paradise from Conder Green down to Cockerham Sands in the south. Swans and ducks live in the canal basin.

Glasson Dock
The Bridge c1965 G260049

Glasson Dock Bridge connects the two halves of the village. Because of its weight restrictions, many of the lorries going in and out of the dock had to go half a mile or more inland before a strong enough bridge could take them over to the West Quay. The bridge today has been rebuilt and strengthened to take the heavy traffic, and is fitted with traffic lights. West Quay was always the visitors' favourite, with its ice cream shop, cafe, fresh fish shop and the Dalton Arms. Today these have been joined by the Kingfisher Studio, with exhibitions by a local artist, and behind the Dalton Arms is the Port of Lancaster's Smoke House with its own production of smoked herring, trout and duck.

Around Lancaster

People dash north and head for the Lake District. Coaches convey thousands of day trippers east to visit the Yorkshire Dales. Both miss what is one of the loveliest and quietest areas of the North of England. It is almost like a huge secret, known only to walkers, nature lovers and those who live there. The Lune Valley to the north-east of Lancaster is truly one of the most unspoilt areas in the north; Pilling Moss lies to the south, Quernmore to the south-east and Overton Moss to the west, and all these areas surround the city with peaceful tranquillity. The great artist Turner appreciated this area, and many of his best paintings are of this part of the country. Ruskin appreciated the countryside surrounding Lancaster, and wrote lovingly of the old villages.

Maybe I should not tell the secret, but keep it, so that the area does not have the problems that the Lake District now faces. Too late - I have told you now. So do go and see for yourself, and then keep the secret from anyone else.

Bolton-le-Sands, General View 1898 41055

The village of Bolton-le-Sands sits astride the A6, four miles north of Lancaster. Our photograph shows both the village churches: the Roman Catholic spire is to the left and the Anglican tower to the right. In the Domesday Book the village was mentioned as 'Bodetone', meaning 'the dwelling house of Botl'. It was 1706 before the name became what it is today, a common old England name. The Parish of Bolton-le-Sands is 5,895 acres in size.

Bolton-le-Sands
The Village c1960 B137022
This photograph shows the old village centre, looking from the Roman Catholic church of St Mary of the Angels. Carnforth Co-operative Society looked after the villagers' grocery needs. (Can you remember your divi number?) The building on the left with the pillars on each side of the door is the Blue Anchor Hotel, and Hall's Sweet Shop and Post Office stands between. Peeping out above the inn is the tower of St Michael's Church, one of the oldest in the district. Though a lot of the church has been rebuilt, the tower is 15th-century; it has three bells in it just as old.

◄ **Bolton-le-Sands, The Catholic Church 1898** 41059
Here we have the old centre of the village, now by-passed by the main road. The Roman Catholic church of St Mary of the Angels with its free-standing spire dominates the centre of our photograph. Catholics started meeting in a barn in 1868, and this church was consecrated in 1884. The hotel on the left is the Blue Anchor Hotel; the name reminds us how near the sea is, only half a mile behind Wild Duck Farm. There has been an inn on this spot since 1706.

▼ **Bolton-le-Sands The Canal c1960** B137030
This peaceful view shows the Lancaster Canal as it passes through Bolton-le-Sands. There is not much evidence of the Swinging Sixties in our photograph. The canal arrived here in 1797, and transformed the village into a town. Between 1820 and 1849, passenger boats on the canal were the main form of transport between Kendal and Preston, and the Packet Boat Hotel, seen here, was one of the inns built for passengers so that they could eat on their journey or wait for the next boat. The inn's name reflects this: the boats were called Packet Boats, and carried letters and parcels as well as people.

◄ **Bolton-le-Sand Shore Road c1965** B137034
This is the road down to the shore (and Red Bank Farm). Red Bank is one of the spots from which you can cross the sands over to Kents Bank. In Victorian times, Bolton was a favourite spot for those who wanted a quiet peaceful holiday, and it became a welcome means of making money for the locals to take in visitors. Horse-drawn coaches and wagonettes would come from Morecambe and Lancaster, and local children would meet the visitors and sell them snacks and bunches of flowers.

▼ **Brookhouse, The Village c1955** B872003
Brookhouse is an ancient village north-east of Lancaster just above Caton. It is at a junction on the old Caton to Claughton road, which we can see going off to the left. The inn on the right is the Black Bull, and Leslie Speckling was landlord at the time. The five hundred-year-old parish church tower of St Paul's shows up at the top of our photograph.

Brookhouse The Village c1955 B872058 ►
We are looking up Tern Brook, which runs off Caton Moor and gives the village its name. St Paul's tower is at the top of the photograph. The church also boasts a Norman doorway. The old stone bridge over the Tern Brook is from early times as well, and marks the division between Brookhouse and neighbouring Caton. The brook runs into the Lune at a spot called Crook of Lune, one of the most charming parts of the river.

▲ **Caton The Druids' Oak c1955** C473013
Our caption says Caton, which is correct, but only just: the wall to the left is the bridge over Tern Brook, and the houses we see are actually in Brookhouse. In front of the ancient oak are a set of steps known locally as the Fish Stones. History tells us that they were built as a counter and shop; here the monks from Cockersands Abbey brought salmon and other fish they had caught in the River Lune to sell to the villagers. Only monks were allowed to catch salmon, and the money they raised paid for their needs and candles. The oak tree has a preservation order on it.

◄ **Cockerham**
The Village c1955 C599010

Cockerham, the village and Cockersands, the Abbey, both take their names from the River Cocker, which runs between them. Cockerham today is not actually on the river, which runs across the large Cockerham Moss. In the Domesday Book it is written as 'Cocreham'. The original village was burnt down in the 1600s and had to be completely rebuilt. The villagers left the burnt-out village and moved on to the main road, around the Manor Inn, seen here in our photograph. Just the church of St Michael remains in its original position, away in the fields.

J.R. BROCKBANK
BOOKSELLER, STATIONER,
GENERAL
PRINTER & BOOKBINDER.
CARNFORTH
WOOL SHOP
Wm YATES & Co
C MACDONALD
WATCH MAKER

Carnforth Market Street 1898

41032

Carnforth, six miles north of Lancaster, has a place in history as a railway town. The Furness & Midland Railway and the London & North Western Railway opened Carnforth Station between them in 1880, and it was always an important junction. For nearly twenty years the ex-British Rail depot here was the Steam Town Railway Preservation Centre, but this closed down in the early 1990s. Wolstencroft, the chemist's on the right of photograph, is worth a close look. The board above the entrance boasts that they serve General Drugs and Patent Medicines, Horse & Cattle Medicines and Thorleys Cattle Spice, as well as being Oil & Colour Merchants. They were also agents for the Caledonian Fire & Life Insurance and Ocean, Railway & General Accident. They sold sleeping powders, cures for influenza and butter colour. They even advertised 'Teeth Carefully Extracted' - this is reassuringly etched into the glass door.

▼ **Halton, From The River c1955** H506010
At the time of the Domesday Book, Halton was the main administrator of the area, and Lancaster was 'under' Halton, which lies three miles north-east of Lancaster. The River Lune runs south of the village, which has Saxon and Roman remains under today's sprawling housing estates. In the Domesday Book it was spelt as it is today; the name comes from either 'halgh', an ancient word for hill, or from an Icelandic invader named Hella who settled here.

▼ **Halton, The Church c1960** H506052
Here we have a close-up view of Halton Parish Church, St Wilfred's, and the rectory next to it. There has been a church on this spot since Norman times. The one we see here was rebuilt in 1877, but the tower was left alone and dates from 1597. Like many other churches round here, it possessed three bells, one of them as old as the tower. There are three Anglian cross shafts of the 8th and 9th century in the churchyard, and worked into the walls of the tower are many old stones and remnants, including a Roman altar to the god Mithras. The two-storied vault of the Bradshaw family is here, among the treasures of this ancient place of worship.

▲ **Halton, The River Bank and the Bridges c1960** H506055
The River Lune has never suffered the amount of industrial pollution that its southern Lancashire sisters the Mersey and the Ribble have had. Here we see youngsters enjoying swimming and paddling in the river. The two bridges that cross the river here can be clearly seen in the background. Castle Hill is the highest spot in Halton, and this hill, above the church, is the place where Roman, Saxon, Danish and Norman defences have once stood.

◀ **Hest Bank, The Canal c1955** H453003
Hest was part of Bolton-le-Sands, and was a hamlet near Morecambe Bay. Hest Bank was the seaward side of the village, right at the southern side of the mouth of the River Kent. At one time, the area was referred to as Slyne with Hest. The Lancaster Canal Act was passed in 1792; the canal from Kendal to Carnforth opened first in 1797, and then this section opened, Bolton-le-Sands via Hest Bank to Lancaster. As soon as the canal opened, it proved an easier and more comfortable way of travelling and moving goods than along the poor roads that existed at the time. Packet (passenger) boats, barges and pleasure boats all used the waterway from the very outset.

Hest Bank, Station Road c1955 H453001
Station Road led down to the railway station, now long gone. They called the main railway line from Crewe to Glasgow the West Coast Main Line, but here at Hest Bank is the only spot where you can actually see the coast and the sea beyond. Hest Bank is the name used for the whole settlement. Three forms of transport have cut through the area at various times: the main Roman road, later the A6, the Lancaster Canal, and the railways, all bringing prosperity and extra work to the area. The railway was so busy a century ago that a footbridge was built so that visitors did not have to wait to cross the line to get to the beach. We can see this bridge in our picture at the bottom of the road.

Hest Bank, The Centre c1960 H453016
This is the A6 cross-roads, with 'Halt' signs painted on the road and squared T-shaped traffic signs gently controlling what little traffic there was. There are no yellow lines, no posts everywhere with instructions and restrictions - oh, it was such a gentle time for motor travel. The name Hest comes from 'hyrst' (a copse or wood), and the name was first recorded in 1184.

Hornby
The Castle c1910 H454020

'A picturebook castle' is how the castle at Hornby has been described. Painted by the artist Turner, it became famous and was much visited. It was built by the Norman Montbegon family just after they arrived in Lancashire. They lived in the motte and bailey Castle Stede nearby while it was being constructed. Later it was owned by the Harrington family, who lost both father and son and heir in a Civil War battle. An uncle took the castle from the female line of the family, and they had to plead with the King before it was restored to them. One daughter married into the powerful Stanley family, and the castle passed to them. It was Sir Edward Stanley who led the Lancashire men at Flodden Field. He was created Lord Monteagle for his bravery. One later owner was Colonel Charteris, who became wealthy after cheating at cards. Then it belonged to a rich financier called Pudsay Dawson, and the Foster family owned it when our photograph was taken. It is still a private residence today.

▼ **Lancaster, The Canal 1918** 68332
This picture of peace and tranquillity, though it was taken in 1918, could really have been taken in 1998 or even yesterday. Note the boathouse on the far bank. I wonder if these people were charged every time they used the canal, or if they paid a one-off or annual fee. In March 1895, the canal drained overnight owing to subsidence, and washed away the surface of Station Road, Hest Bank. Note the white paint on the bridge archway to make it stand out on dark winter mornings or in twilight.

▼ **Overton, The Post Office c1960** O121008
The parish of Overton lies five miles south-west of Lancaster on the road to Sunderland Point. Tucked away in a very secluded corner below Heysham, this little village was mentioned in the Domesday Book as Ovretun; the name turns up very frequently in old documents, usually mentioning the church or a curate. The lovely old church here still retains its original Norman doorway. Overton means 'dwellings by (next to) the water', and the village used to flood at every high spring or autumn tide.

▲ **Over Kellet**
The Village 1923 74161
Over Kellet is a village off the main road, on the Arkholme road out of Bolton-le-Sands. Here we see the two monuments in the village centre. The nearest is the old village cross, and the new white pillar beyond it, with the railing round it, was at this time the newly-erected memorial to those who never returned from the Great War in 1914-18. Later the old cross was turned into a memorial for the Second World War. The 'Over' part of the name means upper, or northern, and the Kellet part means roughly 'hill of the spring'. Above the village is Pedder Potts reservoir, which is said to be named after a local poacher, and beyond that is Lord's Lot Wood.

Quernmore, The Crossroads c1955 Q17503
The village of Quernmore is three miles south-east of Lancaster. Quernmore Park Hall lies just over a mile north of the village. A quern was a Roman hand-mill, and the moor behind the village had the ideal material to make these small mill-stones. Kvernberg is Old Norse for a mill-stone quarry. The village took its name from the great Quernmore forest which once covered this area. This photograph shows the cross-roads, where the motorist could get some refreshment and petrol in those days of more leisurely travel. The road behind us climbs up to Hare Appletree Fell.

Warton Crag 1898 41041
As we head north, Warton Crag is the first sign of the Lake District with its ancient limestone rocks. Behind Warton Crag the Lake District really builds up its thrusting and stark peaks, softened over time with the water catchments that led to the lovely lakes. The village of Warton, shown here, lies sheltered beneath the Crag and looks peaceful, but it was a hard-working place to live in a century ago. Copper mining was one of the local industries, though farming was the main source of employment.

Warton, The Village 1897 40501
The village of Warton lies by the River Keer seven miles north of Lancaster on the A6. It is a parish of 11,000 acres, plus 8,000 acres of sandy shoreline when the tide is out. There were gravel diggings in the area, and from them, Pine Lake was created alongside the village. Warton is famous for its American connections. Ancestors of George Washington built St Oswald's Church, seen in the middle of our photograph. The family crest contained stars and stripes, and these were used as the basis for the American flag. The stars and stripes of the USA is flown every 4th of July in the village. Thomas Washington, one of the last of this branch of the family, was vicar here from 1799 to 1823. Washington House, where the Washington family lived, still stands in the village today.

Index

Frith Book Co Titles

www.frithbook.co.uk

The Frith Book Company publishes over 100 new titles each year. A selection of those currently available are listed below. For latest catalogue please contact Frith Book Co.

Town Books 96pp, 100 photos. County and Themed Books 128pp, 150 photos (unless specified). All titles hardback laminated case and jacket except those indicated pb (paperback)

Around Bakewell	1-85937-113-2	£12.99
Around Barnstaple	1-85937-084-5	£12.99
Around Bath	1-85937-097-7	£12.99
Berkshire (pb)	1-85937-191-4	£9.99
Around Blackpool	1-85937-049-7	£12.99
Around Bognor Regis	1-85937-055-1	£12.99
Around Bournemouth	1-85937-067-5	£12.99
Brighton (pb)	1-85937-192-2	£8.99
British Life A Century Ago	1-85937-103-5	£17.99
Buckinghamshire (pb)	1-85937-200-7	£9.99
Around Cambridge	1-85937-092-6	£12.99
Cambridgeshire	1-85937-086-1	£14.99
Canals and Waterways	1-85937-129-9	£17.99
Cheshire	1-85937-045-4	£14.99
Around Chester	1-85937-090-x	£12.99
Around Chichester	1-85937-089-6	£12.99
Churches of Berkshire	1-85937-170-1	£17.99
Churches of Dorset	1-85937-172-8	£17.99
Colchester (pb)	1-85937-188-4	£8.99
Cornwall	1-85937-054-3	£14.99
Cumbria	1-85937-101-9	£14.99
Dartmoor	1-85937-145-0	£14.99
Around Derby	1-85937-046-2	£12.99
Derbyshire (pb)	1-85937-196-5	£9.99
Devon	1-85937-052-7	£14.99
Dorset	1-85937-075-6	£14.99
Dorset Coast	1-85937-062-4	£14.99
Down the Severn	1-85937-118-3	£14.99
Down the Thames	1-85937-121-3	£14.99
Around Dublin	1-85937-058-6	£12.99
East Sussex	1-85937-130-2	£14.99
Around Eastbourne	1-85937-061-6	£12.99
Edinburgh (pb)	1-85937-193-0	£8.99
English Castles	1-85937-078-0	£14.99
Essex	1-85937-082-9	£14.99
Around Exeter	1-85937-126-4	£12.99
Exmoor	1-85937-132-9	£14.99
Around Falmouth	1-85937-066-7	£12.99
Around Great Yarmouth	1-85937-085-3	£12.99
Around Guildford	1-85937-117-5	£12.99
Hampshire	1-85937-064-0	£14.99
Around Harrogate	1-85937-112-4	£12.99
Around Horsham	1-85937-127-2	£12.99
Around Ipswich	1-85937-133-7	£12.99
Ireland (pb)	1-85937-181-7	£9.99
Isle of Man	1-85937-065-9	£14.99
Isle of Wight	1-85937-114-0	£14.99
Kent (pb)	1-85937-189-2	£9.99
Around Leicester	1-85937-073-x	£12.99
Leicestershire (pb)	1-85937-185-x	£9.99
Around Lincoln	1-85937-111-6	£12.99
Lincolnshire	1-85937-135-3	£14.99
London (pb)	1-85937-183-3	£9.99
Around Maidstone	1-85937-056-x	£12.99
New Forest	1-85937-128-0	£14.99
Around Newark	1-85937-105-1	£12.99
Around Newquay	1-85937-140-x	£12.99
North Devon Coast	1-85937-146-9	£14.99
Northumberland and Tyne & Wear	1-85937-072-1	£14.99
Norwich (pb)	1-85937-194-9	£8.99
Around Nottingham	1-85937-060-8	£12.99
Nottinghamshire (pb)	1-85937-187-6	£9.99
Around Oxford	1-85937-096-9	£12.99
Oxfordshire	1-85937-076-4	£14.99
Peak District	1-85937-100-0	£14.99
Around Penzance	1-85937-069-1	£12.99
Around Plymouth	1-85937-119-1	£12.99
Around St Ives	1-85937-068-3	£12.99
Around Scarborough	1-85937-104-3	£12.99
Scotland (pb)	1-85937-182-5	£9.99
Scottish Castles	1-85937-077-2	£14.99
Around Sevenoaks and Tonbridge	1-85937-057-8	£12.99
Around Southampton	1-85937-088-8	£12.99
Around Southport	1-85937-106-x	£12.99

Available from your local bookshop or from the publisher

Frith Book Co Titles (continued)

Title	ISBN	Price
Scottish Castles	1-85937-077-2	£14.99
Around Sevenoaks and Tonbridge	1-85937-057-8	£12.99
Around Southampton	1-85937-088-8	£12.99
Around Southport	1-85937-106-x	£12.99
Around Shrewsbury	1-85937-110-8	£12.99
Shropshire	1-85937-083-7	£14.99
South Devon Coast	1-85937-107-8	£14.99
South Devon Living Memories	1-85937-168-x	£14.99
Staffordshire (96pp)	1-85937-047-0	£12.99
Stone Circles & Ancient Monuments	1-85937-143-4	£17.99
Around Stratford upon Avon	1-85937-098-5	£12.99
Sussex (pb)	1-85937-184-1	£9.99
Around Torbay	1-85937-063-2	£12.99
Around Truro	1-85937-147-7	£12.99
Victorian & Edwardian Kent	1-85937-149-3	£14.99
Victorian & Edwardian Maritime Album	1-85937-144-2	£17.99
Victorian & Edwardian Yorkshire	1-85937-154-x	£14.99
Victorian Seaside	1-85937-159-0	£17.99
Warwickshire (pb)	1-85937-203-1	£9.99
Welsh Castles	1-85937-120-5	£14.99
West Midlands	1-85937-109-4	£14.99
West Sussex	1-85937-148-5	£14.99
Wiltshire	1-85937-053-5	£14.99
Around Winchester	1-85937-139-6	£12.99

Frith Book Co titles available Autumn 2000

Title	ISBN	Price	Month
Cotswolds (pb)	1-85937-	£9.99	Sep
Cornish Coast	1-85937-163-9	£14.99	Sep
County Durham	1-85937-123-x	£14.99	Sep
Dorset Living Memories	1-85937-210-4	£14.99	Sep
Dublin	1-85937-	£9.99	Sep
Herefordshire	1-85937-174-4	£14.99	Sep
Kent Living Memories	1-85937-125-6	£14.99	Sep
Leeds (pb)	1-85937-202-3	£9.99	Sep
Ludlow (pb)	1-85937-176-0	£9.99	Sep
Norfolk (pb)	1-85937-195-7	£9.99	Sep
North Yorks	1-85937-		Sep
Somerset	1-85937-153-1	£14.99	Sep
Surrey (pb)	1-85937-		Sep
Tees Valley & Cleveland	1-85937-211-2	£14.99	Sep
Thanet (pb)	1-85937-116-7	£9.99	Sep
Tiverton (pb)	1-85937-178-7	£9.99	Sep
Victorian and Edwardian Sussex	1-85937-157-4	£14.99	Sep
Weymouth (pb)	1-85937-209-0	£9.99	Sep
Worcestershire	1-85937-152-3	£14.99	Sep
Yorkshire Living Memories	1-85937-166-3	£14.99	Sep
British Life A Century Ago (pb)	1-85937-213-9	£9.99	Oct
Camberley (pb)	1-85937-222-8	£9.99	Oct
Cardiff (pb)	1-85937-093-4	£9.99	Oct
Carmarthenshire	1-85937-216-3	£14.99	Oct
Cheltenham (pb)	1-85937-095-0	£9.99	Oct
Cornwall (pb)	1-85937-229-5	£9.99	Oct
English Country Houses	1-85937-161-2	£17.99	Oct
Folkestone	1-85937-124-8	£9.99	Oct
Humberside	1-85937-215-5	£14.99	Oct
Manchester (pb)	1-85937-198-1	£9.99	Oct
Norfolk Living Memories	1-85937-217-1	£14.99	Oct
North Yorks (pb)	1-85937-		
Preston (pb)	1-85937-212-0	£9.99	Oct
Reading (pb)	1-85937-238-4	£9.99	Oct
Salisbury (pb)	1-85937-239-2	£9.99	Oct
South Hams	1-85937-220-1	£14.99	Oct
Suffolk (pb)	1-85937-221-x	£9.99	Oct
Swansea (pb)	1-85937-167-1	£9.99	Oct
West Yorkshire (pb)	1-85937-201-5	£9.99	Oct
Around Aylesbury (pb)	1-85937-227-9	£9.99	Nov
Around Bradford (pb)	1-85937-204-x	£9.99	Nov
Around Chichester (pb)	1-85937-228-7	£9.99	Nov
East Anglia (pb)	1-85937-265-1	£9.99	Nov
East London	1-85937-080-2	£14.99	Nov
Gloucestershire	1-85937-102-7	£14.99	Nov
Greater Manchester (pb)	1-85937-266-x	£9.99	Nov
Hastings & Bexhill (pb)	1-85937-131-0	£9.99	Nov
Helston (pb)	1-85937-214-7	£9.99	Nov
Lancaster, Morecombe & Heysham (pb)	1-85937-233-3	£9.99	Nov
Peterborough (pb)	1-85937-219-8	£9.99	Nov
Piers	1-85937-237-6	£17.99	Nov
Wiltshire Living Memories	1-85937-245-7	£14.99	Nov
Windmills & Watermills	1-85937-242-2	£17.99	Nov
York (pb)	1-85937-199-x	£9.99	Nov

See Frith books on the internet www.frithbook.co.uk

FRITH PRODUCTS & SERVICES

Francis Frith would doubtless be pleased to know that the pioneering publishing venture he started in 1860 still continues today. A hundred and forty years later, The Francis Frith Collection continues in the same innovative tradition and is now one of the foremost publishers of vintage photographs in the world. Some of the current activities include:

Interior Decoration

Today Frith's photographs can be seen framed and as giant wall murals in thousands of pubs, restaurants, hotels, banks, retail stores and other public buildings throughout the country. In every case they enhance the unique local atmosphere of the places they depict and provide reminders of gentler days in an increasingly busy and frenetic world.

Product Promotions

Frith products are used by many major companies to promote the sales of their own products or to reinforce their own history and heritage. Frith promotions have been used by Hovis bread, Courage beers, Scots Porage Oats, Colman's mustard, Cadbury's foods, Mellow Birds coffee, Dunhill pipe tobacco, Guinness, and Bulmer's Cider.

Genealogy and Family History

As the interest in family history and roots grows world-wide, more and more people are turning to Frith's photographs of Great Britain for images of the towns, villages and streets where their ancestors lived; and, of course, photographs of the churches and chapels where their ancestors were christened, married and buried are an essential part of every genealogy tree and family album.

Frith Products

All Frith photographs are available Framed or just as Mounted Prints and Posters (size 23 x 16 inches). These may be ordered from the address below. From time to time other products - Address Books, Calendars, Table Mats, etc - are available.

The Internet

Already twenty thousand Frith photographs can be viewed and purchased on the internet. By the end of the year 2000 some 60,000 Frith photographs will be available on the internet. The number of sites is constantly expanding, each focussing on different products and services from the Collection.
The main Frith sites are listed below.

www.francisfrith.co.uk
www.frithbook.co.uk

See the complete list of Frith Books at:

www.frithbook.co.uk

This web site is regularly updated with the latest list of publications from the Frith Book Company. If you wish to buy books relating to another part of the country that your local bookshop does not stock, you may purchase on-line.

For further information, trade, or author enquiries please contact us at the address below:

The Francis Frith Collection, Frith's Barn, Teffont, Salisbury, Wiltshire, England SP3 5QP.
Tel: +44 (0)1722 716 376 Fax: +44 (0)1722 716 881 Email: uksales@francisfrith.com

See Frith books on the internet www.frithbook.co.uk

To receive your FREE Mounted Print

Mounted Print
Overall size 14 x 11 inches

Cut out this Voucher and return it with your remittance for £1.50 to cover postage and handling, to UK addresses. For overseas addresses please include £4.00 post and handling.
Choose any photograph included in this book. Your SEPIA print will be A4 in size, and mounted in a cream mount with burgundy rule lines, overall size 14 x 11 inches.

Order additional Mounted Prints at HALF PRICE (only £7.49 each*)

If there are further pictures you would like to order, possibly as gifts for friends and family, purchase them at half price (no additional postage and handling required).

Have your Mounted Prints framed*

For an additional £14.95 per print you can have your chosen Mounted Print framed in an elegant polished wood and gilt moulding, overall size 16 x 13 inches (no additional postage and handling required).

*** IMPORTANT!**
These special prices are only available if ordered using the original voucher on this page (no copies permitted) and at the same time as your free Mounted Print, for delivery to the same address

Frith Collectors' Guild

From time to time we publish a magazine of news and stories about Frith photographs and further special offers of Frith products. If you would like 12 months FREE membership, please return this form.

Send completed forms to:
The Francis Frith Collection, Frith's Barn, Teffont, Salisbury, Wiltshire SP3 5QP

Voucher for **FREE** and Reduced Price Frith Prints

Picture no.	Page number	Qty	Mounted @ £7.49	Framed + £14.95	Total Cost
		1	**Free of charge***	£	£
			£7.49	£	£
			£7.49	£	£
			£7.49	£	£
			£7.49	£	£
			£7.49	£	£
Please allow 28 days for delivery				*** Post & handling**	**£1.50**
Book Title				**Total Order Cost**	**£**

Please do not photocopy this voucher. Only the original is valid, so please cut it out and return it to us.

I enclose a cheque / postal order for £ ....
made payable to 'The Francis Frith Collection'
OR please debit my Mastercard / Visa / Switch / Amex card
(credit cards please on all overseas orders)

Number ....

Issue No (Switch only) .... Valid from (Amex/Switch) ....

Expires .... Signature ....

Name Mr/Mrs/Ms ....

Address ....

....

....

.... Postcode ....

Daytime Tel No .... Valid to 31/12/02

The Francis Frith Collectors' Guild

Please enrol me as a member for 12 months free of charge.

Name Mr/Mrs/Ms ....

Address ....

....

....

.... Postcode ....